I0085261

Stoplights Are For Singing

Easy Ways to Bring More Harmony to Your Family

BONNIE B. DANEKER

Illustrated by Eevie Lanier

Stoplights Are For Singing: Easy Ways to Bring More Harmony to Your Family

Bonnie B. Daneker, author

Copyright ©2024 The Author's Greenhouse, LLC

First Edition

All rights reserved. Reproduction of the whole or any part of the contents, without written permission from the publisher, is prohibited. For rights or permissions inquiries, please contact the author, Bonnie B. Daneker at bonnie@theauthorsgreenhouse.com

ISBN: 978-0-9773785-8-6 (Paperback)

ISBN: 978-0-9910032-3-5 (eBook)

Illustrations by Eevie Lanier

Book design by Becky's Graphic Design®, LLC

www.BeckysGraphicDesign.com

Printed in U.S.A

To my family of origin, my family by marriage, and my family of choice. Some harmonize better than others, but I love you all.

How This Book Began

Over my lifetime, I have met very few people with seven siblings from the same parents, like me. It's true, I'm one of eight kids! I'm Number 6, in case you were curious.

In our home—which was seldom empty—everyone shared rooms (until the older ones eventually moved out), and everyone did chores. We worked hard and studied hard. It was very important to our parents that we got along and played together. We did have a lot of fun: outdoor sports, indoor board games, nature walks, creative time, cooking traditions and baking experiments (plus clean up!), as well as singing together were all de rigueur. We had enough people for two teams to play, or make, or do just about anything. As a result, we understood the importance of both spending time with each other and spending time alone, too.

In the process of growing up, we learned about helping out and doing really thoughtful, loving things for each other. This book references many of the activities we shared. While it's rare to have a family as big as mine in the same household, most people can identify with having a brother, a sister, aunts, uncles, or grandparents. It's my hope that these thoughtful gestures bring harmony and connection to you and your family as they did for ours.

With Love, Bonnie B. Daneker

P.S. By all means, make these ideas your own! Send in other suggestions or comments to me on the Stoplights Book Series Facebook page.

Stoplights
Are For Singing

1
Sing at the stoplight

On our regular visits to the grandparents, all 10 of us would
pile into the station wagon. We would travel 300 miles there
and back, cramped tightly in the three rows of seats. Sleeping
or playing games occupied us until, undoubtedly, we would
get antsy for the long trip to be finished. My parents would
distract us by urging us to sing "Downtown," "Up, Up and Away,"
or "99 Bottles of Beer on the Wall" (which would keep us busy
for a long time). Singing brings a sense of camaraderie and
fun, and this memory makes me smile. The next time you're
in the car together, consider belting out a favorite tune.

2

Hold hands

When my younger brother came home from the hospital, he was so tiny—just over 4 lbs. His twin was not stable enough to come home at the same time. I saw my chance to bond early with this little guy and tried immediately to hold him. He was too fragile, I was told. The best I could do is reach between the slats of his little crib and try to have him grab my finger. He connected instinctively. Even as adults, we need to hug or hold hands with our siblings. When we're on good terms, there is a closeness that is beyond compare.

3

Make bathtime fun for babies and tots

Teaching children early about keeping clean is important, and how better to do it than by making it fun! Brick-and-mortar stores and online shops feature a stunning variety of bathtime toys, bright rubber duckies, and sudsy scrubbies. As we watch a little one in our family grow, it's curious to see what she is interested in as she ages—and what she can handle from a viewing, dexterity, and learning perspective as older siblings or friends share toys with her.

4

Visit international markets

When our family went to the international market to shop for food, the boys had never been to a store this size or kind. It served up so many strange sights and smells! After introducing them to global varieties of familiar foods like breads and chocolates, they were more willing to try foreign sauces, meats, and vegetables. That experience opened them up to discovering new food at grocery stores or restaurants, many they now love to eat.

5

Share family photos

One of the first things people notice when visiting a friend's home is the presence (or lack thereof) of family photos. It's a joy to see how people interact with each other and how they change over time. A popular way to display snapshots is to string them across the room. In the days of digital, another clever way to display is to upload them to a shared drive— an especially useful tool for connecting across the miles!

family trip!

wedding day!

alex's 1st!

Snack Chart
M TU W Th F Sat Sun
Chips & Dip
Watermelon
Fruit Gummies
Granola bar
String cheese
Cooking Schedu

6

Make your "Snack Calendar"

Most people have a snack of choice—M&Ms®, gummies, or potato chips, to name a few. Stocking everyone's favorites can require more time or money than we may have. One family I know has a Monthly Snack Calendar to track the snack choice of one child per week. Each time they grocery-shop, they consult the calendar on which bag or box to buy for the week. Everyone has a turn to have their favorite during the month.

7
I.D. clothes

In kindergarten, I learned the value of names on your clothes. We were listening to our teacher read when—with a *Bang!*—the rack of hooks in the back of the room fell down with its heavy weight. We had uniform gym clothes and very similar coats, and it took time to sort out belongings. Luckily, my coat was labeled with my name—then I just had to locate my unlabeled gym clothes! When siblings have similar clothing at home, it is easier to tell the difference when you put your names or initials on with fabric paint, a patch, or a Sharpie® marker.

8
Get chewy vitamins

In the days before yummy gummies, we would take supplements with a little dread. Vitamin C was sour. Vitamin D was chalky. Vitamin E was fishy, and cod liver oil was . . . well, cod livery. It's become a pleasure to take supplements as they are often disguised with cherry, watermelon, grape, and orange flavors. With a little chew, you can feel like you're eating a sweet treat instead of a good-for-you supplement. If some in your family has trouble taking supplements as pills, a gummy-type chew could be a good substitute.

9

Keep curfew

Though younger children may balk at early bedtimes and teenagers may balk at curfews, setting standard times for rest is important to every part of their lives. Sleep studies let us know that the body repairs and recharges with regular, consistent sleep. Studies also show that more accidents and crime happen at night. When parents put curfews in place, it's to keep their children safe.

10
Keep the first aid cabinet ready

"No one gets to adulthood without a few scraps or bruises," they say. One of the best ways prepare for these is to stock a first aid kit or cabinet (or both, if you can). We are prepared for the flu, colds, upset stomachs, and other common maladies with some of our favorite medicines at home. We keep a variety of adhesive bandages and other supplies in each car. Having these items ready avoids some last-minute runs to the store when you can spend your time giving comfort to the sick or injured person instead.

11
Honor birthdays

Say, "I'm glad you were born!" with thoughtful words and gestures on their birthday. If their favorite food is ice cream, for example, find a way to enjoy it with them. Consider giving "experience gifts," like movie passes or putt-putt gift cards to do together. If experience gifts aren't a possibility, remember to call, send a thoughtful email or text. My brother recently sent one that made me laugh aloud: "Let me be the first to wish you Happy Belated Birthday and Happy Early Birthday next year!!" He is helping me continue the celebration and I love it.

HAPPY BIRTHDAY!

12

Make haircut appointments together

Barbershops—though becoming increasingly rare—have been centers of community for many years. Men come to the barbershop not only for cuts and shaves, but also as a social time to catch up with friends or family. It is often seen as a "rite of passage" to have your first visit to the barber, marking a special time in a boy's life. Usually, a father or uncle takes the child for his first cut, but sometimes big brothers go, too. It's extra fun when you can get your hair cut with someone you know and trust, especially if it's your first time.

13

Replenish craft supplies

We were encouraged to be creative growing up, and almost every room in our house had supplies to make or enhance something: paints and brushes; coloring books, pencils, and crayons; fabrics and threads; glitter and glue. If you have a crafty area of your home, take a look regularly at your supplies. When you notice materials that are running low or used up, it's a nice gesture to fill, replace, or add it to the list of supplies to replenish so that it's ready for the next person to use.

14

Gift a "Laundry Coupon"

Teenagers in general don't love doing laundry. One father recounted asking his son to put his dirty clothes in a box in the corner of his room until he was ready to clean them. It grew so smelly—and his inventory of clothing decreased so dramatically—that the boy finally gave in and walked down the hall to the laundry room for a few loads. Family members can make coupons "good for one free load of laundry" as a special reward for something done well, like a high grade in a tough subject or a volunteer effort.

15

Get out their PJs

For small children especially, planning what to wear to sleep can be great fun. If you have multiple choices, you can coordinate their PJs to what season it is (lighter fabric for warmer days, heavier for cooler ones), what book you're reading, what holiday it is, or what clothing you have in common.
For example, a neighbor would want to dress in her "Frozen" sleepshirt after she and her mom watch the movie together. When you start preparing for bedtime like that, it is less of a struggle to get them down (when they think it's their idea).

16

Help out at their school

My in-laws loved to help out at athletic events and school fundraisers for their grandchildren. Sometimes they would volunteer at the concession stand. Sometimes they would bring a crock-pot full of chili to warm up hungry players and parents after the game. More often, they would support bake sales by preparing brownies, cookies, or muffins. They always seemed to be contributing something, making sure that we all knew they cared and wanted to be part of our lives.

17

Make a new summer concoction

With several thirsty kids around, there was always some creative mixing of ingredients to make interesting flavors of punch and other soft drinks. We combined Kool-Aid® and Gatorade® mix, squeeze bottle flavors with pixie sticks, or melted freezer pops with lemonade. The colors often turned out as interesting as the flavors. Occasionally, we would create a really good one that we would try to mimic again, like strawberry lemonade or grape-lime juice (which had a great taste but awful color).

18

Wash or iron a special outfit

Some people could not envision my intelligent, accomplished, and artistic older brother behind an ironing board, let alone ironing a special dress for his little sister. Yet I have a permanent picture of this in my mind, because he helped me getting ready for an important event—lunch with him at a very swanky restaurant for my 14th birthday. As we get older, we can assist our younger relatives in looking their best because, chances are, we've done it before! This goes not only for siblings but also visiting grandparents, and aunts and uncles, who generally enjoy being useful during their stays.

19

Create secret codes or symbols

For secrecy or game playing, communicating in another "language" between family members can be just plain fun. Whether you create something unique or use something already available but not widely known (like pig Latin, invisible ink, or basic substitution), codes and symbols can be useful in puzzle solving or scavenger hunts. The more people you share them with, the wider your playing group can become. Or, you can keep it small and have a super-exclusive club.

20

Take advantage of outdoor fun

Celebrate the season with good clean fun. In geographies which are fortunate enough to have four seasons, kids can engage in playful games based on the weather. Have winter fun by throwing snowballs or building forts with freshly-fallen flakes. Play "Tag" or chase fireflies in the cool spring evenings. Cool off by playing water-balloon-catch or chasing each other over the sprinklers during the summer. Jump in piles of fall leaves after you've raked them up (but before you have to bag them). As the seasons change, the opportunities to have fun within them changes too, so enjoy them while they last!

21

Sing holiday songs together

On Christmas Eve, when siblings were "home" at our parents' house from college, travels, or their own homes, my parents gathered us around the piano for some indoor Christmas caroling. Each child sat on the piano bench and played a carol—individually or duet. Then my parents took turns plowing through the song books, nearly in their entireties. The snow outside buffered some of the singing, but I'm sure the neighbors could have heard us loudly singing, "Jingle Bells," "12 Days of Christmas," and "He's Got The Whole World (In His Hands)."

22

Cook their favorite dinner

On our parents' Date Nights, we were allowed to plan our dinner menu and cook it, as long as we cleaned up. The older ones prepared what the younger ones wanted. Nutrition was optional, as we ate Pigs in a Blanket, mac-n-cheese (with any number of protein add-ins), frozen pizza (with optional toppings like hot dogs), and popcorn. We'd wash it all down with some semblance of an ice cream float. Energized, we'd do the dishes during TV commercials, then we'd go to sleep in our rooms before Mom and Dad got home. It was a win-win for everyone.

23

Spice up your tooth care routine

Brushing and flossing teeth can be viewed as dreaded tasks, even though most of us like a beautiful smile. Consumer products companies have come up with new products to keep it interesting. For a change, try out a different flavor—like cinnamon or licorice—or color—like red and white swirl—in a sample-size. Get one for your sibling when you are trying it for yourself. The shared experience can keep you connected with a clean, winning smile.

24

Do their chore graciously

Have you ever heard your parents say, "You can't go until you finish washing the dishes!" (or another chore that's your responsibility.) Suddenly, you're scrambling to rinse jars before recycling, putting away dishes "not really dirty" and throwing the rest of the pots and pans in the sink when your sister comes over. She's like an angel when she says, "I'll do this for you, if you're running late" without saying "It'll cost you!" If you have the chance to assist your sibling out when he or she is in a bind, do so without bringing it up or telling them that "You owe me one!"

25

Make them a play list

They say, "Music is the universal language." What music do you share with brothers, sisters, and friends? What are your go-to upbeat songs? Your favorite movie or TV show themes? It's fun to create a list of top music picks, especially if you have a theme or direct purpose. For example, are you making a collection of favorites to just enjoy with friends? Or are you choosing marching songs to practice cadence for your cross-country running team? Music can put you in a great frame of mind no matter the activity.

26

Be quiet when they're trying to nap

My father suffered from terrible migraine headaches, made worse by exposure to bright light and loud noises. When he laid down and shut the door, we kids knew to entertain ourselves in the quietest of ways. If he could rest in silence, the headaches would eventually go away. We did NOT bang on the piano, prepare dinner, or play board games. Instead, we read, folded laundry, or drew. What are your favorite pastimes that can be done quietly indoors? The whole house might appreciate a break from the noise.

27

Keep athletic gear together

Our boys played football, baseball, and basketball, sometimes requiring multiple clothing changes and different gear in a single day. After coming home, belongings were often scattered around the house. It was difficult to find the right jersey or uniform component later—was it in the wash, in the car, in a backpack, or somewhere else? Older siblings can show younger ones how to prepare for the next day's practice or game: the night before, hang them up or have them arranged all in one place so they're ready to go.

28

Carry in school projects

It's almost a given that students will have a large homework project that requires more than two little hands to bring into the classroom. From science projects to scout badges, kids may need larger, stronger hands to carry oversize boards or boxes. This can be a great bonding moment between a child and older siblings or grandparents, where the projects are described as well as how they were made— while making a memory between the two of you.

29

Form an internet research club

When we were growing up and had questions, our parents
often encouraged us to "look it up in the dictionary" or
"find out what the encyclopedia says." These days the
amount and type of questions children ask may be similar,
but the researching methods are advanced. Kiddos now
huddle around computers, with whoever's got the fastest
computer and typing fingers driving. Parents or older
siblings and relatives can suggest searches for youngsters
to explore, from "how-to" videos to book summaries.

30

Explore the attic together

Attics can be dark, frightening places. They can also be full of mystery and excitement with unusual clothes, picture albums, or interesting furniture. Scary movies have been known to start with a scene featuring two kids going up the stairs to the attic—but magical ones do, too. If it's safe and clean—and kiddos have the permission to investigate—they may be curious to look around. It can be a fun organizing project for them, and they may find things they want to keep like retro T-shirts, vintage jewelry, or components for a Halloween costume.

31

Go to doctor's appointments with them

No matter what age you are, doctor appointments can be upsetting. When you're a child, you likely have little to no experience with medical professionals. In the waiting room, it can be reassuring to have brother or sister with you, especially one whom has just been through what you're about to experience (like shots or a physical exam). Grandparents can be especially calming if they have been through several rounds of having children in pediatric offices (and they often know which have good toys or treats for kids).

32

Drive younger siblings to where they need to go

It is always an occasion to celebrate when a 16-year-old gets a new driver's license. In our house, with so many kids, we celebrated because there was another person to play chauffeur. Older, licensed siblings drove around those of us who had after-school events or other errands. My oldest sister had a VW Beetle and she could pack six of us in at one time, with one small sibling riding in the "cubbyhole" way back seat.

33

Make your parents breakfast in bed

Let Mom and Dad sleep in on the weekends, holidays, or a special day (like their anniversary), then make breakfast. Two easy meals are a bowl of cereal or seasonal berries and yogurt, which you can quietly make if your parents are light sleepers. If they are heavy sleepers and you have some confidence in your culinary skills, you can reach for the mixing bowl and frying pan to cook pancakes. Flip classic buttery ones or decorate with whipped cream and chocolate chips for an extra treat they will savor.

34

Talk

When kids share rooms, one of the benefits is having your own afternoon or nighttime discussions, particularly when you don't want others to hear what you're saying. You're so close by that you can quietly ask, "Can you talk?" or "Are you awake?" Typical topics of conversations might include their latest crushes, new video games, or which outfits to wear on "Spirit Day." It's understandable why bunkbeds are still so popular with kids—they can lean over the rails to look at each other and better hear the whispers.

35

Teach shoe care

"You never have a second chance to make a first impression," as the saying goes. Many people overlook the condition of their shoes when getting dressed, but it is an important part of overall appearance. Look at your shoes before you wear them and after you wear them (when you first come home) to determine what they need. Replace broken laces with new ones. Put stinky athletic shoes in the washing machine. Rinse off muddy boots in the sink after gardening or playing in the rain. Waterproof and polish dress shoes. Caring for them will lengthen their life and make you look better.

36

Let a littler one win

Ready, set, go! Who hasn't run a race against a parent, brother or sister? The simple contest of trying to "best" them before they get to a tree, dock, or sidewalk is free and entertaining, except when one person is always the loser. Every so often, let the younger, smaller, or slower one win. There may be a fine line between building confidence and indulging a child in athletics, but give it a try for their sake. Even if you don't win, you'll still get some exercise in while enjoying the time together.

37

Keep your bikes ready to ride

———————————————

Bikes with "banana seats" were a staple in our neighborhood. These could "grow with you" because you could scootch back on the triangular seat to reach the pedals as your legs lengthened. You could also put two on a seat, one riding in front and one in back. While it may not have been 100% safe (or parent-approved), it was great fun to ride around together. This usually happened when one bike wasn't in working condition (flat tire, broken chain, bad brakes), so we did our best to keep all of our rides in tip-top shape.

38

Wink

There are times, as siblings, that you don't need to say a word. Like the times we know what Mom and Dad would say. Or how a movie ends. Or when you know what was supposed to be your surprise gift. Nonverbal communication is viewed as more powerful than verbal communication because it is quick and efficient, and is rarely misunderstood. It's something siblings—and especially twins—have with each other that outsiders may not understand. Use those signals—a wink can be worth hundreds of words.

39

Share clothes

Not everyone views hand-me-downs as fun, especially when you are the third or fourth to have worn it. However, when you're the second one and you've so coveted your sister's new blouse, or your brother wants his older brother's designer polo, it's another story. A fun idea is to put together a rack of outgrown clothes—either within your family or between families—and see if there is interest from different members as they choose their own, like shopping. Good for the environment and your budget!

40

Vacuum out the family car

What can we find on the floormats or under the car seats? Crushed Goldfish® or Cheerios®, escaping french fries, or fast-moving grapes, right? We regularly washed our cars at home, before there was a car wash in town. As we were vacuuming the interior, we would stretch the hose to get into every nook and cranny. If some coins or other treasure was found by the vacuumer, it became their property. It's nice to sit in a clean car, but it's even nicer when you discover a treasure!

41

Take care of the pets

Usually, one child or parent ends up taking the responsibility for a pet, but it is a good idea to share it. When schedules conflict with regular feeding or medical care, the pet can suffer. If you bring home a kitten, for example, divvy up the duties: Make a fun home with play toys and climbing items just for her. Fix a litter box and change it regularly. Give her good food and clean water. Brush her and trim her claws. Take her to the vet for check-ups, vaccinations, or dental care. Most of all, give her tons of affection.

42

Fix something that needs repairing—without them asking

Are you the person in your family to whom others turn for repairs? The one with "magical tools" and talent to fix jewelry, patch tears, or replace lost buttons? You may be asked constantly to work your "magic" to restore things to "good as new" condition if those around you are really active. Instead of dreading it when they ask, anticipate it—like noticing a broken necklace on their dresser—and take the initiative to fix it before they have a chance to ask you, just to be nice.

43

Let them have the last cookie

While some homes have a "no-sweets" policy, others have
sweets around for every meal. Ours was more of the latter,
complete with a pig-shaped cookie jar. Hungry kiddos,
especially teenagers, will often argue who gets the last of
any food—especially if someone has baked a fresh batch.
Our favorites were sugar cookies, crispy marshmallow
treats, and peanut butter bars. If there is an opportunity
to give away the last treat—no matter how badly you
want it—consider doing it. They may turn around and split
it with you, or let you have the last one the next time.

COMPOSITION BOOK

Olivia

44

Decorate with customized stickers

Do you remember getting ready for the first day of school? Getting new school supplies is so exciting! We all wanted to personalize our folders and composition notebooks so we could tell them apart (when so many were floating around the house). We used colored markers or pens to make designs all our own. If you're getting—or making—stickers for yourself, get a few extras for your brother or sister to customize their supplies. Adding a bit of color and splash can be energizing for both of you.

45

Capture a special moment

Spaghetti seems to be a favorite food for little ones—fun to eat, fun to play with, and fun to wear. One of my favorite pictures is a snapshot capturing a moment when all three were happening. While it's fun to be in the action and create these moments, it can be even more fun to step back and capture them instead. It's so easy now to take pictures, with cameras in our phones, that there's almost no reason not to. And if you're quick, you just may get to both pose with the little one in a selfie and get one of her all on her own.

46

Give them a pep talk

School athletics are important to many families, especially when it's a big event. We all know it's easier to "get your game face on" when your head's in the game. A soccer goalie might not feel ready without his special gloves—and a reminder of how he blocked key goals in the last games. A football tackle might not feel ready without putting face paint under his eyes before he puts on his helmet—and a word of encouragement from his coach. Sending them off with a little pep talk can both provide support and ease their nerves.

47

Play games

Who would guess that 64 squares could hold so much entertainment value? We would play checkers and chess for hours: at home, on long trips, at relatives' houses, and even with our neighbors! Young and old could be engrossed in a game while others watched. With the lightweight, foldable boards and plastic checkers or chess pieces, it was easy to tote around. We often played round-robin, with the winner sitting for another game against a new opponent.

48

Go swimming

A favorite childhood memory of my husband's is swimming with his sisters. It's easy to envision the three of them among neighborhood kids in a pond or lake, maybe laughing and jumping off a tire swing. Hunting for tossed coins, holding your breath, or playing "Marco Polo" are some of the games they played. Swimming in the summer sun seems to be a classic memory for families around the world.

49

Learn about trees

A homework assignment for a grade-school science class was learning 20 types of trees and collecting leaves from each. In understanding their differences, we also learned how they grew and what their needs were for soil, water, and light. If you're fortunate enough to have trees where you live (in your front yard, for example), take care of one. Look up what type it is and how it grows best. Trim it, weed around it and rake up the leaves when they fall. If you don't have trees nearby, volunteer to tend the trees for a needy neighbor, sports field, or church.

50

Bring in groceries

You can imagine how much food a big family eats. Weekly grocery store trips required a lot of work. My mom primarily made the list, shopped, and brought the groceries home, and we kids helped bring them in and put them away. As we got older, we went to the store with her, then for her, as we were able to drive. Try to anticipate when your parent or sibling comes home from the store to assist them in bringing in the goodies. Put them where they need to be, so everyone can find them when they're hungry!

51

Share lessons you've learned

Fractions, square roots, polynomials—Oh My! The complexities in mathematics can be difficult to grasp. You may be more of a "word" person and not understand "numbers" as well as your older brother, who whizzed through trigonometry. Asking for tutoring when they "get it" and can explain in a way you get it, too, can be priceless. You may be able to return the favor when they have an English composition paper due and they are struggling with dangling modifiers, compound sentences, or source citations. Sharing your strengths in doing schoolwork is a special benefit of having siblings.

$$-5(x-5)=50$$
$$-5x+25=50$$
$$-25-25$$
$$\frac{-5x}{-5}=\frac{25}{-5}$$
$$x=-5$$

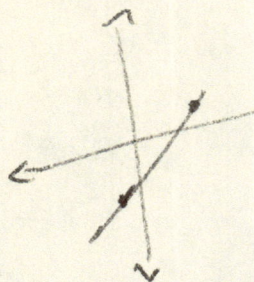

$$3(m-6)=6$$
$$3m-18=6$$
$$+18+18$$
$$\frac{3m}{3}=\frac{24}{3}$$
$$m=8$$

52

Say, "You're a great brother" or "You're a great sister," and mean it.

We often say this sort of thing with qualifiers or in jest, but the sentiment takes on a special significance when you really mean it. Set aside some quality time for each other. Put quibbles aside and really talk to each other. Recreate something you did as kids. Pop a tent with sleeping bags in the back yard, even as adults, and reminisce about the good times. Whether they are part of our family of origin, family of marriage, or family of choice, make sure to tell them you love them and are glad you're in each other's lives.

About the Author

A lifelong learner and writer, Bonnie B. Daneker has been part of the publishing industry for more than 20 years. She established Georgia's first publishing advisory firm to help clients write books and has managed over 100 book-content projects.

Before her time in publishing, she worked in technology consulting. Bonnie holds a BA in Journalism from The Ohio State University, an MBA in Strategic Planning and Entrepreneurship from The Goizueta Business School at Emory University, and the Sustainability Associate Certification from ISSP. She has instructed at Savannah College of Art and Design (SCAD) and guest-lectured at Emory University. Bonnie lives with her husband outside Dallas, TX.

Visit her website at www.TheAuthorsGreenhouse.com

About the Illustrator

A "digital painter," Eevie Lanier is a book and visual development illustrator. She has done work for Square Panda and Stride educational video games.

Eevie is a graduate of Savannah College of Art and Design(SCAD) with a BFA in Illustration with a Concentration in Concept Design for Animation and Games. Previously, she graduated from the Alabama School of Fine Arts. She lives in Birmingham, AL with her two dogs and one cat.

She can be reached through LinkedIn at: www.linkedin.com/in/Eevie-Lanier.

More from
Bonnie B. Daneker:

Stoplights Are For Kissing

Stoplights Are For Laughing

Leave a Review!

As a self-published author, reviews mean the world! Please leave a review on the platform from which you purchased this book. I read every one!

www.ingramcontent.com/pod-product-compliance
Lightning Source LLC
Chambersburg PA
CBHW061136030426

42334CB00003B/55

* 9 7 8 0 9 7 7 3 7 8 5 8 6 *